Bygone
BRENTWOOD

EAST END of ST THOMAS' CHURCH
BRENTWOOD
ERNEST·C·LEE ARCHITECT

ST THOMAS' BRENTWOOD

Bygone
BRENTWOOD

John Marriage

Phillimore

1990

Published by
PHILLIMORE & CO. LTD.
Shopwyke Hall, Chichester, Sussex

ISBN 0 85033 740 2

Printed and bound in Great Britain by
BIDDLES LTD.
Guildford, Surrey

List of Illustrations

Illustration Acknowledgements

The author wishes to thank the following for permission to reproduce photographs: Brentwood School, 1, 16, 68, 78, 82-89, 126, 165; Chelmsford Museum, 141-43, 152, 154; Mrs. Chown, 134, 150; Mr. T. Cumbers, 178; Mrs. A. Dan, 177; Essex Bus Enthusiasts Group, 111-19, 125; Jon Ellis, 4, 13, 17, 20, 21, 23, 25, 26, 32, 42, 62-64, 70, 72-76, 81, 94, 96, 103, 104, 121, 122, 128, 131, 132, 144, 145, 155, 173; Essex County Police, 164, 171; Essex Record Office, 12, 55, 56, 58, 59, 67, 126, 130, 148, 174, 176; Mrs. G. Griffith, 157, 163; Herongate and Ingrave Preservation Society, 28, 39, 48, 49, 57, 60, 61, 101, 102, 158, 159, 167a, 167-69, 175; Ilford Ltd., 98-100, 123, 124; Stan Jarvis, 137, 150; Henry and Joan King, 46, 129, 139; Great Eastern Railway Society, 170; Lloyd's Bank plc, 5, 166, 120; Locomotive Club of Great Britain, 108, 110; NatWest Bank plc, 11, 65; Miss N. C. Savill, 160-62, 172; L. Whittaker, 2, 3, 6-8, 14, 15, 19, 22, 27, 29, 30, 35, 38, 40, 41, 43, 44, 47, 52, 95, 105, 106, 109, 127, 135. All other material is from the author's collection.

Preface and Acknowledgements

Although I have lived within a mile of the current boundaries of the Brentwood District for a quarter of a century, much of my knowledge of the area was limited to what was visible from the window of the car or train in which I passed each day on my way to work. When the opportunity came to research and produce this book I did so with great pleasure, as it enabled me to learn much more about the history of this fascinating and attractive area, so near to London but in places still very rural.

I received considerable help from very many people in the preparation of the book and in particular I would like to thank Miss Nancy Savill and Miss Barbara Phillips of the Ingrave and Herongate Museum and Record Office, Mr. Ian Hook of the Essex Regiment Museum at Chelmsford, Mr. Alan Osborne of the Essex Bus Enthusiasts Group, Mr. John Evans, Headmaster of Brentwood School, and Mr. & Mrs. Jon and Mabel Ellis. Finally, I must thank my wife, who cheerfully corrected the grammatical and spelling errors and made a great many valuable suggestions on the general layout and content.

Introduction

Administratively, Brentwood District is modern. Prior to the end of the last century Brentwood was only a small hamlet within the ancient parish of South Weald. In 1897 the Brentwood Urban District was formed and consisted of a mere 460 acres on either side of the present Brentwood High Street, south-east of the Ongar/Ingrave Road junction. This enclosed most of the built-up area then existing, although new development was already beginning to spill over into the adjoining parts of Shenfield, Great Warley and South Weald parishes. The population of the little community was then about 5,000. In the 1930s, as a result of rapid expansion in the whole of south Essex, there was a general review of local authority boundaries. South Weald was detached from the Romford Rural District. Similarly, the parishes of Great and Little Warley, Shenfield, Ingrave, East and West Horndon and Childerditch were taken from the former Billericay Rural District and all were brought together to form a greatly enlarged Brentwood Urban District, with about 28,000 people. As a result of local authority changes in the 1970s, Ingatestone, Mountnessing, Blackmore and Doddinghurst were added and the whole area became the present Brentwood District, with a total population of about 74,000. Ecclesiastically, the Roman Catholic Church has always been strong in the District and today Brentwood is the seat of the diocese.

Nowadays, the main built-up area extends in the form of a cross from Brook Street to the south-east of the original town, beyond Shenfield to Hutton in the north-east, and from Pilgrims Hatch in the north-west to Ingrave Green in the south-east. In the early post-war years both East and West Ham built large garden estates on the west side of the town which consolidated the earlier development. Some villages, like South Weald and Great Warley, retain a very quiet and rural appearance and are little changed outwardly from earlier times, whilst others, such as Doddinghurst, Kelvedon Hatch and Ingatestone, have greatly expanded.

The original town, whose name is said to be derived from 'Burntwood', was founded on the important crossing of the London to Colchester and Harwich road with the Ongar to Tilbury road, once part of an important pilgrim route over the Thames to Canterbury. In 1227 a market was granted at this point and the town grew alongside. Even now a particular feature is the long, broad and straight High Street, where market trading once took place. Later, when the London to Colchester road became an important turnpike, Brentwood was a major coaching stage. The many inns provided overnight accommodation and a change of horses for this traffic and the private carriages and gigs also using the road. Horse-drawn traffic reached its zenith in the mid-19th century but was soon lost to the newly constructed Eastern Counties Railway, which also acted as a spur to the major development of the town as a growing number of City employees settled there, travelling to work by train to Liverpool Street Station each day. Many new houses and villas were built near the railway station and so the developed area gradually expanded.

Villages

Ingatestone, another old market town, also lies on the ancient highway from London to the coast. In earlier times it was considerably larger than Brentwood and also an important coaching stage, with numerous inns. It is believed that its name derives from three large Sarsen stones – one at either corner of the High Street/Fryerning Lane junction, and the other in the churchyard – hence 'Ing-atte-stone'. Unlike Brentwood, it still retains most of its quaint old buildings which still flank the narrow, almost straight High Street, following the route first established by the Romans. In 1850 Ingatestone had a population of about 1,600 and like Brentwood it has now expanded to become a dormitory community, with the majority of its people working either in London or Chelmsford. Most of the traditional industries such as maltings have now been swept away and replaced by modern housing.

The village has its place in medical history as Dr. Sutton lived and practised there. He pioneered inoculation of cow-pox serum in the fight against the fatal and disfiguring disease of smallpox. No.98 High Street, an attractive Georgian house adjacent to the market place, may be where his surgeries were held.

Ingatestone Hall stands just outside the village. The present building dates back to 1548 when it was built by Sir William Petre, who purchased the manor from the Crown. He built the Hall to a quadrangular pattern with an inner courtyard nearly 100ft. square but later the western range of buildings was demolished, leaving the courtyard open. His son, Sir John Petre, bought Thorndon Hall, built by James Paine in 1770, which became the family's principal house until it was damaged by fire in 1878. Part of the building has recently been restored and converted into high quality flats. After the Great War the family returned to Ingatestone Hall. Sir William Petre also constructed, in 1557, several almshouses in Stock Road, but most were demolished to make way for the railway in 1840 and replaced by 12 almshouses in Roman Road built to a mock-Tudor style. These have recently been renovated. In accordance with the original trust deeds, residents must be 'practising Roman Catholics, over the age of 50 and in need'.

Although a windmill still exists at Mill Green, it has been disused for many years. A more prominent landmark is the one at Mountnessing. Built in 1807, this has a red brick roundhouse base, which once had a thatched roof. Above is the buck, the wooden upper section, to which the sails are fixed. This rotates to face the wind, and the power from the sails is transmitted to turn the mill stones. Towards the end of the century it was supplemented and then replaced by a steam mill which was erected nearby. However, milling ceased before the last war and the steam mill was demolished. With the passing of the various Town Planning Acts after the war, the windmill became a Listed Building and was subsequently restored by enthusiasts.

Blackmore is a pleasant village nestling around a green. The church of St Lawrence, a short distance away, is of Norman origin and a very substantial building indeed, constructed from the outset with aisles. It was once part of a priory, dating back to 1155, and has one of the most impressive timber towers in England. In 1527 the priory was dissolved and all the other monastic buildings have now disappeared. The remains of a ring road, reputedly created at the time of the Black Death, skirt the village, and today's traffic still uses part of it.

The attractive twin villages of Ingrave and Herongate are to the south-east of Brentwood, astride the old pilgrims' route to Canterbury. Although many older buildings remain, giving character to both villages, considerable suburban-type development took place in the early post-war years. St Nicholas' church at Ingrave is described by Pevsner as the most remarkable 18th-century church in the county, having a massive tower widened by recessed polygonal turrets, which rise above its parapet.

Other large villages within the District include Doddinghurst and Kelvedon Hatch, both of which expanded greatly during the inter-war period.

Commerce

Like most market towns on former coaching routes, both Brentwood and Ingatestone had a wealth of public houses in Victorian times, providing the only liquid refreshment which was both safe and relatively cheap. Most of the inns were of ancient origin and Brentwood had more than average because of the large numbers of soldiers permanently based at Warley. It has been estimated that at one time in the last century there were ten inns on the north side of Brentwood High Street and nine on the south, as well as others along Kings Road and Warley Hill. At Ingatestone, too, there were coaching inns. A substantial number have survived but one long mourned disappearance is the *Spread Eagle*, replaced, sadly, by shops. The number of inns and public houses has fallen steadily throughout this century and many have been either demolished or converted to other uses as trade declined with the growth of alternative forms of entertainment. The pubs within walking distance of Warley Barracks, in particular, suffered a huge loss of trade when the barracks closed in the 1960s. Most villages, though, have at least one 'local' and there is still a good choice in the main Brentwood town area.

Some of the brews were locally produced at Hills Brewery, off Myrtle Road, or Fielders Brewery in Kings Road. Other beers came from further afield, like Wells and Perry's Brewery in Duke Street, Chelmsford, or Ind Coope from Romford.

The Victorian era saw the establishment of the modern banking system and branches of national banks began to open in the town. The London and County Bank opened a branch in 1852 and then moved to purpose-built premises costing £4,700 in 1885. Today, the same site is occupied by the National Westminster Bank, a successor company. The National Provincial Bank opened a branch in 1927 in Lester House but closed following its merger with Nat West in 1971. A few years previously, in 1921, Midland Bank opened on its present site, whilst Lloyds Bank arrived in Brentwood in 1938. In 1883 the so-called 'Essex Bank' opened a branch in Brentwood. This bank was founded in 1801 by Crowe, Sparrow and Brown at Chelmsford and was later absorbed by the present Barclays Bank.

Brentwood High Street has long been a centre for retail trade, many of the properties being converted from private houses. Today, many are branches of national chain stores but earlier this century almost all the shops were owned by individual proprietors who either lived above the shop or, if they were prosperous and successful, in villas elsewhere in the town or in one of the nearby villages. As well as tailors, chemists, drapers and grocers, the shops represented trades long gone such as hatters and coopers. Providing for the substantial military presence was another aspect of commercial life. Probably the best known shop in the town was Wilsons, the large departmental store at the junction of Shenfield Road and Ingrave Road. It was destroyed by fire on 4 September 1909 but was afterwards rebuilt. Ingatestone, and to a lesser extent Blackmore, too, once boasted a wide variety of shops but the range has steadily reduced due to competition from larger centres.

The 1930s and '40s were the golden age of the screen, when cinema-going was a weekly event for most people. There were three cinemas in Brentwood. The Parade, something of a 'flea pit', was near the railway station, whilst the Electric Palace and the Odeon were both in High Street. The latter stood behind the ruins of St Thomas the Martyr and was demolished to make way for the present shopping precinct. The site of the Parade is now occupied by offices. A dual-screen cinema within the shopping precinct provides for present-day film buffs.

Education

Brentwood School, one of the oldest public schools in the country, was founded in 1558 by Antony Brown, Serjeant at Law, who lived at Weald Hall. Shortly after its foundation he became Chief Justice of Common Pleas and the author of a treatise which helped to ensure the succession of James VI of Scotland to the throne of England. The school was originally free to all boys who could read and write and who lived in any of the 17 parishes of which any part was within three miles of the school. In 1825 the Charity Commissioners intervened and free tuition was given only to Latin and Greek scholars. All else had to be paid for.

The school has been through difficult times. In 1852 it was at a low ebb, with only 45 boys attending. However, it took on a new lease of life in 1881 when Edwin Bean, who previously had experience in Australia, was appointed headmaster. In 1893 a new scheme was set up to manage the school with two of the 13 governors being appointed by Essex County Council and scholarships were granted to boys from council elementary schools. Gradually the number of pupils picked up. Many of the children made use of the developing rail network to get to school each day. They were known as 'trainboys'. As the numbers of pupils increased more staff were needed as well as additional buildings. The Society of Old Brentwoodians and other benefactors provided funds for the main buildings, erected in 1907. Development continued, with further buildings being added but during the two world wars a halt was called.

After 1946 more State and County scholarships were made available, with the result that more boys stayed on to sixth form courses and then gained places at university. By this time the number of pupils had increased to nearly one thousand. The school remains popular today and can boast continuing distinguished scholastic achievements.

In addition to the main school there is, of course, also the preparatory school. Originally Roden House was used both as the preparatory school and as the main school boarding house. In 1946 boarders were moved to Old House and the preparatory school moved to the Hermitage in 1947. Roden House is mow the headmaster's residence. In 1949 the preparatory school moved to Middleton Hall, once the home of Countess Tasker.

The Brentwood County High School for Girls was founded by Miss Kate Bryan as one of several private dame schools in the district. She built, in 1876, a three-storey detached property at the corner of Queens Road and Rose Valley, named Montpelier House. It quickly became very successful, achieving high academic results and consequently attracted an ever increasing number of pupils. In the early part of this century Essex County Council decided that a girls' secondary school was required in Brentwood and so in 1913 they purchased a site near Shenfield Common. However, the Great War postponed construction and so they took over Miss Bryan's school as the County High School, appointing her the first headmistress. The new school buildings were opened in 1927. Once established on the new site, the school continued to expand with further buildings being added from time to time. Montpelier House continued to play its part in serving the community, becoming the Brentwood Health Clinic.

The Ursuline Sisters from Forest Gate, East London, were invited in 1900 by the local Roman Catholic clergy to start a convent school in Brentwood. Mother Clare purchased a house called Matlock in Queens Road for the purpose and it was soon enlarged due to a rapidly increasing school roll. Adjoining properties were also acquired. Later, the school moved to its present location at the junction of Queens Road and Eastfield Road. Nevertheless, two former houses – Bleak House and Fairview – still form part of the complex of buildings. The present cloakrooms in Eastfield Road were the Assembly Hall and the present dining room was the gymnasium in the days when there were only 60 pupils.

The school expanded, with St John's block built in 1912, the swimming pool in 1924 and the Hall and Trinity Block in 1939. However, Trinity Block was hit by incendiary bombs in September 1941 and not repaired until 1951, although the school continued to function as best it could. Throughout the war the Sisters themselves housed and tended the fire crews who defended East London, whilst local people sheltered in the cellars beneath the Hall. Further building has taken place in the post-war years, and by damming a small stream a lake was created to the south. Although totally independent at first, the Ursuline Convent High School became a Direct Grant Grammar School in 1920 but it is now a Voluntary Aided School for Girls with a boarding unit for 60.

In Victorian times the churches played a prominent part in the provision of elementary education. The Church of England founded National schools, whilst the Nonconformists ran British schools. Thus, the School of Christ Church, Great Warley, was built in 1846 on land which had once been owned by the East India Company and was later acquired by the War Department. Other schools included St Paul's at Bentley Mill, and Shenfield, later St Mary's, which both opened in 1864.

From 1835 to 1867 the former chapel of St Thomas the Martyr, now a ruin, was used as a National Boys School. When the building was declared unsafe, new schools were erected in 1869 in Love Lane, now Coptfold Road. Other Church schools were opened at Mountnessing, South Weald, and Ingatestone. Later, the local authority began to play an increasingly important part, building its own schools. Great emphasis was placed on the 'three Rs' – Reading, (W)riting and (A)rithmetic. Emphasis on classroom discipline meant that standards in these early elementary schools were surprisingly high, even if the classes were large and the buildings often primitive and cramped. The Education Act of 1944 brought sweeping changes: existing elementary and Church schools mostly became County primary schools, senior schools were enlarged and the school leaving age raised by stages to 16 so that all children received secondary education, not just the fortunate few. Today, keeping pace with the growing population, there are a large number of primary and secondary schools within the District.

Open Spaces

Warley Place, a 16-acre site, now designated as being of special scientific interest and leased to The Essex Naturalists Trust, was once occupied by a substantial mansion dating back to Queen Anne's time and surrounded by gardens and parkland. From 1875 to 1934 it was the home of Miss Ellen Willmott, a keen horticulturist responsible for introducing to Warley, and the British Isles generally, many exotic plants.

Under Miss Willmott's guidance extensive landscaping took place. Several ponds, once reputedly used as fish lakes by Barking Abbey, were converted into water gardens. Completing the setting was an alpine hut, with mountain furniture and herdsmen's gear which she brought from Bourg St Pierre. Napoleon, it was said, spent the night in this hut whilst crossing the Alps in May 1800 on his way to Milan. It was re-erected in Warley Place beside the ponds and near an Alpine wild garden, with a stone bouldered gorge, creating a 'rushing water' effect.

The many rare trees and shrubs, estimated at over 100,000 different species within the grounds, as well as the walled garden, greenhouses and cold houses, kept the 104 gardeners busy from dawn to dusk. Although open on only one day of the year to the public, Miss Willmott showed her gardens to friends in the R.H.S. and eminent gardeners from all over the world. Among Miss Willmott's friends was Sir Thomas Hanbury, who himself created a garden of tropical plants near Ventimiglia in Italy. She supported his expeditions to China from where she acquired many specimens. Many plants from Kew Gardens were sent to Warley for trials.

Long before her death, the enormous cost of the undertaking began to eat into Miss Willmott's capital, for as well as Warley she had other houses on the Continent. The garden began to decay and after her death was plundered for its rare plants. A property developer purchased the estate in 1938 and the house was demolished the following year. After the war the now derelict site, with its ruined gardens, became part of the Green Belt and so remained undeveloped. Although reverting to woodland, with some of its introduced trees and plants surviving, the site was eventually leased to the Essex Naturalists Trust who now maintain it as a nature reserve.

Although there are many well landscaped parks and open spaces within the District, Thorndon Park deserves special mention. Once the estate comprised 3,500 acres, surrounding Thorndon Hall.The present 400-acre country park is designated as a site of Special Scientific Interest. Originally designed by Capability Brown in the 17th century, the country park includes ancient woodland, deer pasture, hay meadows and ponds all rich in wildlife. In addition, a substantial area of land is now an attractive and well used golf course, reputedly one of the best in the county.

Weald Park is another large open space, also a country park. It was purchased jointly by the Essex County Council, the London County Council and the Brentwood Urban District Council in the early 1950s. Weald Hall, a glorious old house in beautiful gardens, once stood within the grounds. It was used on occasions as a monastic retreat and a royal residence. Georgian in appearance, it had Elizabethan origins. Unfortunately, after a fire during World War Two, it was demolished. Once it was the residence of Sir Antony Browne, the founder of Brentwood School, who in 1558 also built and endowed the Weald Almshouses to provide accommodation for the deserving poor of Brentwood. Weald Park has a lake, woodland and the remains of a large Iron Age encampment originally covering about seven acres. The park was an ornamental enclosed deer park until 1945, when troops assembled there in preparation for D-Day. The surrounding fences were breached by vehicles and all the deer escaped into the surrounding countryside. Some flourished and wild fallow deer are now common in the area between Brentwood, Abridge and Ongar. However, other species in the park, Red, Japanese Sika and Roe, are thought not to have survived.

Industry

The Brentwood district has no great tradition of industry, most of the land dominated by agriculture. The small towns of Brentwood and Ingatestone were able to satisfy most of its industrial needs. At Brentwood there were several maltings and breweries, a brick works near the site of the railway station, and the engineering firm of W. J. & C. T. Burgess in Ongar Road, which made a wide variety of agricultural machinery. This firm was founded in mid-Victorian times under the names of Burgess and Key, closing in 1923 when the buildings were taken over by A. E. Symes Ltd., the London building contractor.

At Ingatestone there was a maltings and a large agricultural merchant but both have now been replaced by housing.

In recent times a number of large office blocks have been constructed at Brentwood. Since the mid-1960s Ford has had its European headquarters at Warley. Nevertheless, most residents in the district continue to commute to Greater London, with the exception of those employed in service industries and shops.

Brentwood did, however, play a substantial part in the early development of the telecommunication industry. The rapidly expanding Marconi Company of Chelmsford decided in 1919 to develop and operate a wireless telegraph service. A transmitting station was built near Ongar in 1921, together with a receiving station at Ongar Road, Brentwood. At the same time a large central telegraph office was constructed in Wilson Street, London. This became known as Radio House. In 1922 the Ongar and Brentwood stations, together with Radio House, took over the developing Continental circuits and some transatlantic traffic. The Ongar Road station included a series of huge radio towers. The transatlantic receiving antenna was supported in square formation on four 200-ft. towers. In addition, there were six receivers, each tuned to a different transmitting station, and fed simultaneously from one antenna. The antennae for the Continental circuits were supported on 96-ft. towers. Subsequently the stations were taken over by the Post Office and afterwards by British Telecommunications. Eventually the towers were dismantled.

Rotary Hoes Ltd. played an important part in the mechanisation of British agriculture. Their extensive factory was just within the boundaries of the district, on the north side of the Fenchurch Street railway line and close to the West Horndon railway station. Many of the employees lived in the village, but others came by train each day from places like Southend or Romford. The factory is now used for other purposes.

Brentwood was once home to an important photographic industry, famed throughout the world and of outstanding importance in helping the Allies win the Second World War. In 1899 Ilford Ltd. started to manufacture photographic plates at their factory which was almost completely surrounded by open fields on the banks of the River Roding at Ilford. Soon, however, houses rose from the green fields, their coal fires belching smoke which, when combined with fumes from a gas works on the far side of the river, caused thick winter fogs which damaged the plates in the factory drying rooms. It was decided to build a new factory and, in 1901, eight acres of land were purchased on Great Warley Common and the factory was ready for occupation in June 1904. At the same time, employees' cottages were built in Britannia Road. Despite the move to this more rural and cleaner environment, it proved impossible to equal the quality of the plates made at Ilford. Eventually, the problems of atmospheric pollution were overcome at Ilford and in April 1910 Warley was shut down, leaving only a skeleton maintenance staff in occupation.

In 1912 Ilford Ltd. decided to enter the growing roll film market and so imported specialised equipment from Germany and production quickly started at the empty Warley site. This continued until spring 1916 when the Warley factory was requisitioned by the Government for military use. In June 1920 the army moved out and, when the market revived, Selo Ltd. was set up to manufacture roll film, although repairs had to be carried out on the building first. Once production started in 1921, attention turned to making ciné film and in 1923 the first came on the market, with double-sided x-ray film following.

As a result of the company's success, the parent, Ilford Ltd., decided that all their roll films should be sold under the trademark 'Selo' and the name 'Ilford' was reserved for plates and paper. Amateur photography quickly became very popular and 'Selo' was one of the leading brands of roll film, being sold at most chemists, photographic shops and even through vending machines. During the 1930s Ilford entered into negotiations with an American company to make colour films and a licence was granted in March 1935. 'Selo' colour roll film started production almost immediately and a processing station was established in Brentwood. This type of film was used at the coronation of King George VI in 1937.

Urgent preparations were made in 1939 to cope with the approaching war. Air raid shelters were constructed, extra concrete protection applied to the coating block and all the buildings covered with camouflage paint. The Government regarded photography as an essential weapon of war. Civilian consumption was curtailed and production for military purposes stepped up. Wartime use of the firm's product included aerial reconnaissance by the R.A.F. Night film was in particular demand as the rival firm, Kodak, was unable to match Selo's quality. Although a military target, the factory suffered no damage during the war – apart from a hole in the roof caused by a falling anti-aircraft shell.

In post-war days Ilford decided to drop its various trade names and to concentrate on 'Ilford', retaining only the residual 'Selochrome', later also dropped. In the early 1970s a new factory was built at Basildon to replace various smaller factories. The Ilford plant and the Brentwood factory closed in 1976, though some of the original cottages in Britannia Road still survive. Otherwise nothing now remains of this once important Brentwood industry and today Ilford film, the successor to 'Selo', is made at a modern factory at Mobberley in Cheshire.

Transport

The National Omnibus and Transport Co. Ltd. was the first to operate motorised buses within the Brentwood area, starting a service in 1920. Prior to that time, the only public service had been an ancient horse bus which plied between Brentwood railway station and the *Boars Head*, Herongate. Locally it was known as 'the fever box' because of its resemblance to the vehicle which carried infectious patients to the isolation hospital. Just after the First World War, a short-lived service was provided by a Mr. Thurston who converted an ex-army lorry into a rough and ready bus.

On 18 February 1920 three National services commenced. One ran out to Herongate, a second to the *Thatchers Arms*, Warley, and a third to Ongar. The three routes were served by two buses which were garaged in the yard of the *Yorkshire Grey* in the High Street, with the terminal point at the *Chequers Hotel*. This was later moved to the railway station. However, in 1921 the National withdrew all three services following the establishment of the General Bus Company service from Brentwood through to Stratford Broadway via Romford and Ilford.

The National then introduced a service from Chelmsford, passing through Ingatestone, connecting with the General's London service at Brentwood. These changes were the result of an agreement made between the two companies delineating the respective areas in which they should operate. In Essex, the boundary between the two companies ran through Brentwood. Until 1990 this remained substantially unchanged with London Transport, the successor to 'General', operating routes towards London, and the Eastern National, the successor to the 'National', operating to the east towards Chelmsford, Billericay and Basildon. Express services between London and Brentwood were run by Green Line, a London Transport offshoot. However, in July 1990 the decision was made to split the Eastern National into two companies, with buses operating out of garages at Brentwood, Basildon, Hadleigh and Southend taking the name of Thamesway Buses.

Brentwood's own bus company was the City Coach Company Ltd., with headquarters in Ongar Road. In 1928 it acquired the New Express Saloons Ltd., which pioneered the popular Southend to Wood Green route. The company later acquired several small local bus companies, including the Brentwood and District and Regents Buses, and built up a number of services running out of the town to Ongar, Great and Little Warley, Billericay and Wickford. In February 1952 the business, which by then had a fleet of over 100 vehicles, was taken over by the British Transport Commission which handed the services over to Westcliff on Sea Bus Company. This firm subsequently merged with the Eastern National.

The construction of the Eastern Counties Railway was authorised on 4 July 1836. Work started the following year and by 1843 the track had been built to Colchester. The line opened in stages with the first train to Romford on 26 June 1840, followed by one to Brentwood on 1 July 1840. It was opened as far as Colchester on 7 March 1843 but the first passenger train did not steam into that town until later the same month. The line was later absorbed by the Great Eastern Railway.

The railway was constructed as a double track to a 5ft. gauge, but this was converted to the standard gauge of 4ft. 8½in. between 5 September and 7 October 1844. A particular problem encountered at Brentwood was the steep gradient between the town and Shenfield, Brentwood Bank, which is still one of the steepest on any main line. It necessitated the construction of a deep cutting, with the earth being disposed of on Shenfield Common, resulting in spoil heaps which have survived to the present day and have been known to generations of children as 'The Tips'.

The construction of the railway was opposed by many, particularly local landowners, who objected to the noise and disturbance from the work and later from the trains themselves. Furthermore, the labourers were themselves often disruptive. A particular objector was Lord Petre of Ingatestone Hall, who opposed the line being built through his extensive estate, which still surrounds Ingatestone. He received £120,000 in compensation – in those days an enormous sum. He also insisted that Ingatestone railway station should be built to a style in keeping with that of his nearby Hall.

Ordinary people's lives were considerably enhanced by the new railway. Previously, coal was an expensive commodity, brought into the area via the Chelmer & Blackwater Navigation to Chelmsford or along the River Crouch to Battlesbridge from where it was hauled along the poor roads of the time. In the past, only the wealthy could afford this water-bourne coal but the cheaper rail-bourne coal was within the price range of poorer families. Next to Brentwood railway station was a large goods yard, which encouraged the establishment of a number of industries alongside, including a maltings and the town's gas works. At Ingatestone, too, there was a substantial goods yard, from where the small market town was able to ship its cattle and other farm produce.

As a result of growing commuter traffic, the line from Shenfield to Gidea Park was doubled in 1934 to four tracks, to provide fast and slow services. Considerable engineering work was undertaken, and both Brentwood and Shenfield stations were extensively altered and the huge cutting through Brentwood Bank between the two stations was sliced back to take the additional tracks and concrete restraining walls were built virtually the whole way.

Prior to the Second World War electrification between Shenfield and Liverpool Street had begun but it was halted until after the war and finished in November 1949. More recently this has been extended, in stages, to Southend and Norwich. The present Fenchurch Street to Southend line forms the southern boundary of the district for some distance, with a station at West Horndon. However, the original track from Fenchurch Street was built via Tilbury to Southend in the early 1850s, but the now more important loop via Barking to Pitsea was not built until 1888. In 1912 the line was absorbed by the Midland Railway and operated in competition with the Great Eastern Railway. The latter was subsequently taken over by the London and North Eastern Railway. The early post-war years brought nationalisation and the rivals became part of British Rail and are currently united within Network South East.

The Army

Military associations with Warley go back over 200 years. The Common was first used as a military camp in 1742. During the Seven Years War, the American Wars and the Napoleonic Wars tens of thousands of regular and militia troops were encamped there during the summer months. The celebrated Dr. Johnson visited the camp in 1778, staying under canvas for five days. In 1804 it was decided to make Warley Camp a permanent station. Some 116 acres of land were purchased for £5,400 and barracks were constructed for two troops of horse artillery, accommodation being provided for ten officers and 306 other ranks, with 222 horses. In addition, a hospital was constructed. The first garrison consisted of half a battalion of the Rifle Brigade, the other part being stationed at barracks in Romford. The last cavalry regiment to use the barracks was the Scots Greys in 1832.

In May 1842 the East India Company's accommodation at Chatham became inadequate and it was decided to move the troops from Brompton Barracks to Warley, with the engineers and sappers remaining at Chatham. The Company purchased the barracks and the land for £15,000 with the proviso that the Government would have the first option to purchase, should the Company subsequently decide to leave. The Company immediately carried out extensions and alterations to provide accommodation for 785 recruits and 20 sergeants and new building for the officers. For the first time married family accommodation was provided. Further buildings erected in 1856 enabled 1,120 men to be housed. After training the men were drafted to India and at first they marched to Grays where they were ferried to Gravesend and embarked on to the troopships. After 1854 the newly constructed railways enabled them to travel easily from Brentwood to Tilbury.

After the Indian Mutiny of 1857 the Crown took over the administration of India and the East India regiments were incorporated into the British Army. In 1861 control of Warley Barracks reverted to the War Office, which purchased them for £60,000. Initially, the Royal Artillery were stationed there and subsequently the camp became the base for the 44th (East Essex) Regiment and the 56th (West Essex) Regiment along with the depot companies of the East Essex and West Essex Militia, replacing Colchester as the centre for all County regiments.

The 44th Foot saw service in the Battle of Prestonpans in Scotland and also in North America and later in Egypt and Spain. They also fought in the Crimean and Afghan Wars. Among their battle honours was the Eagle standard of the 62nd Regiment of the French Army, captured on 22 July 1812. This was subsequently adopted as their regimental crest. The 56th Foot were raised in 1755 and known as the 'Pompadours' from the rose purple facings on their uniforms. They saw action in Cuba, Gibraltar and the Napoleonic Wars. For their part in the siege of Gibraltar they were awarded the use of the Castle and Key of Gibraltar as their emblems. In 1881 the two regiments became the 1st and 2nd battalions of the Essex Regiment whilst the Essex Rifles and the West Essex Militia became the 3rd and 4th battalions. The Castle and Key of Gibraltar became part of the regiment's cap badge. The regiment saw distinguished action in the Boer War and both World Wars when they served in most theatres of conflict.

In peacetime the regiment served abroad for long periods. At such times most of the Warley accommodation was occupied by visiting regiments, whose officers had their own mess. This was considerably larger and grander than that of the home regiment. With the outbreak of the Second World War the barracks became the Essex Regiment's Infantry Training Centre and in 1941 also that of the Royal Fusiliers. Throughout the war hundreds of men passed through the gates. Large numbers of nissen huts and other temporary quarters were built to house them. As the war came to an end, members of the Dutch resistance came for training and they formed the nucleus of the new Netherlands Army. Throughout the war there was also a large R.E.M.E. and Royal Ordnance Corps storage depot. The Royal Army Pay Corps occupied nearby Coombe Lodge and the A.T.S. provided important support services. In their way, all were as necessary to the war effort as the infantry training depot.

Warley continued both as a training centre and as a depot for the Essex Regiment for some years after the war. In the early post-war years many young National Servicemen spent their first six weeks of army life there, but in 1960, as a result of post-war cuts in the armed forces, the barracks were closed.

Unfortunately, the 1960s was a time when many irreplaceable buildings, part of the nation's heritage, were ruthlessly destroyed. Most of the buildings at Warley, many of considerable historic interest, were swept away to make way for the present headquarters of the Ford Motor Company, which paid £201,751 for part of the site. The R.E.M.E. depot was redeveloped as the Warley Hill Business Park and the Ordnance Depot became the Council Depot. Only a few buildings, including the chapel and the former officers' mess, survive. Part of the old parade ground is now incorporated in Ford's car park. The Essex Regiment itself became part of the Royal Anglian Regiment. Apart from a few evocative street names like Eagle Way and Gibraltar Close, there is now little to show that Warley once had a garrison of considerable national importance.

The War
During the last war, the Brentwood district lay on one of the main routes for enemy aircraft approaching London. The railway, the barracks and the Selo factory were all tempting targets. During the six years of war over 1,000 high-explosive bombs were dropped within the old urban district, together with 19 flying bombs (doodlebugs), 32 long-range rockets (V2s) and many incendiary bombs and parachute mines. The first high explosive bomb dropped at Goldings, Great Warley, on 23 July 1940, and the last, a V2, at Hutton Park on 27 March 1945, only a few months before the war ended. Two of the V2s landed within Warley Barracks but fortunately caused little damage. In all 5,038 houses were damaged or destroyed and 432 people killed or injured. On one occasion, the main railway line was completely blocked between Shenfield and Ingatestone when a bomb exploded on the track. A steam locomotive was derailed and fell into the hole, killing the driver. For a day or so, whilst repairs were being undertaken, main line trains were diverted via the Dunmow and Braintree branch. In another incident Brentwood station was badly bomb damaged – it was not rebuilt until after the war. The first flying bomb to land within the district fell at Hill Road on 15 June 1944, injuring 10 people. Two houses were destroyed and others badly damaged.

The raiders were not always lucky. On 16 October 1940 a Heinkel He 111 was shot down by a Boulton & Paul 'Defiant' night fighter, from No.264 Squadron R.A.F., crashing near Creasey's Farm, Hutton. Two of the crew bailed out and were captured but two others were killed. Another German plane crashed in Hartswood. Misfortune also befell the U.S.A.A.F.: one of their Dakotas crashed near the Ongar Road, apparently out of fuel.

At Ingatestone, a large part of Mill Green Common and the adjoining woodlands were used for military training purposes and as a storage area for D-Day material. Similarly, Weald Park and other open spaces within the district were used as army assembly areas for D-Day.

Hospitals

The relative proximity of London as well as the pleasant nature of the surrounding countryside has encouraged the establishment of various specialist hospitals within the district. For general care, however, Brentwood had its own cottage or district hospital. Its roots go back to the late 19th century when a cottage with an acre of land on the edge of Shenfield Common was purchased and converted into a cottage hospital. It was rebuilt in 1895 and in 1921 a new wing was constructed as part of a memorial to those who died in the Great War.

In the 1930s a major local fund raising drive was initiated to pay for the rebuilding of the old hospital in Crescent Road, Shenfield, on land donated by Mr. Percy Bayman, a local philanthropist. The foundation stone for the new building was laid by H.R.H. Princess Mary and was opened by H.R.H. Princess Helena Victoria in June 1934. Three wards, for men, women and children, were built, together with an operating theatre and substantial outpatient facilities.

After the last war the newly established National Health Service took it over, with more acute cases normally being dealt with at Harold Wood Hospital. The original building at Shenfield Common subsequently became the Brentwood Maternity Hospital and more recently the Four Oaks single family housing scheme.

Warley Mental Hospital was opened in 1853 on land previously part of the Brentwood Hall Estate and purchased by Essex magistrates for £8,000. This very large Victorian Gothic structure, with extensive landscaped gardens, became the Essex County Lunatic Asylum and served the whole county. It is now run by the N.H.S. St Faiths in London Road is of a more classical design even though it, too, is Victorian. Although there is a substantial nurses' wing, built in the 1930s, most of the complex was part of the Shoreditch Agricultural and Industrial School. Later it became the Hackney Union Branch Workhouse and was afterwards taken over by the London County Council. It, too, is now administered by the N.H.S. and the future of both these hospitals is under review.

In the 1920s the Community of the Daughters of Charity of St Vincent de Paul bought a property in Warley Road, standing in 12 acres of woodland, as a tuberculosis sanatorium for young women. It opened on 8 September 1921 as the Marillac Sanatorium. In the 1950s modern drugs proved so successful in virtually eradicating the disease that the N.H.S. asked the Daughters of Charity to extend their work to take young chronically sick patients. To this end more specialised amenities were needed and in 1963, with the closure of Warley Barracks, they purchased from the War Department the former Visiting Regiments Officers' Mess in Eagle Way and converted it into the present distinguished Marillac Hospital. It now specialises in the treatment of multiple sclerosis. The Hartwood Hospital has now taken over its former Warley Road premises.

Public Services

Brentwood's first gas works were sited in Crown Street, but soon after the arrival of the railway larger works were built adjoining the goods yard, where coal could be delivered. Gasometers were erected alongside and from there a network of underground pipes supplied the townsfolk. Smaller works were located next to the railway goods yard at Ingatestone. Both works were eventually taken over by the Gas, Light and Coke Company Ltd. and linked to the company's larger works at Romford and Beckton, East Ham, with production at Brentwood and Ingatestone being discontinued. Following the nationalisation of the gas industry by the post-war Labour government, the North Thames Gas Board took over responsibility. Present supplies are from the North Sea via trunk mains.

The adoption of electricity for lighting and power was slower to develop than gas. From about the turn of the century, there were a few commercial undertakings and a small number of large houses had their own private electricity generators. Most properties did not receive electricity until the 1920s and '30s when it was supplied by either the Brentwood District Electric Co. Ltd. or the County of London Electricity Supply Co. Ltd. However, many outlying houses and farms were not connected to the supply until the late 1940s when the newly created state-owned Eastern Electricity Board erected power lines to all properties as part of a post-war crash programme.

From its headquarters in Romford the South Essex Waterworks Company was set up in the last century to supply much of the southern part of the county including the former Brentwood Urban District. At first most of the water came from bore holes but by the late 1930s much of it was being supplied from the River Stour on the Essex/Suffolk border, via Abberton Reservoir near Colchester. The local supply came from a pumping station at Great Warley which transferred water from a reservoir to a water tower near the Barracks and piped it to local consumers. Mountnessing and Ingatestone were, however, the responsibility of the Chelmsford R.D.C. The district is now supplied by the Essex Water Company.

No proper sewerage system existed in Brentwood in the last century. Cesspools often drained into open stagnant ditches causing ill health and sometimes death. They were a source of increasing concern and a start was made in 1855 on a small sewerage system which was extended in 1884. A sewerage works was opened in Nags Head Lane, Brooks Street, in 1912. Gradually, similar systems were introduced in outlying villages.

Brentwood's first police station was built in 1851 and was staffed by a superintendent and five constables. It consisted of a two-storey building with cells below. This was a comparatively large force for a town the size of Brentwood but was, no doubt, augmented due to the presence of high-spirited soldiers in nearby Warley. Fourteen years later the staff had expanded by the addition of an inspector and another constable. In 1937 a new police station and magistrates' court was built in London Road, with land for further expansion if required. This station remains in use today. Many of the villages, too, had their own policemen who knew everyone. At Ingatestone the original bobby had a large house in the High Street. Although long since replaced by police houses on the edge of the village, it is still known as Old Police Station.

*   *   *

Since Victorian times Brentwood and the surrounding district has become a popular and prosperous residential area, with attractive houses, many set in their own grounds. The well wooded rolling countryside, sweeping down towards the Thames estuary, is sprinkled with appealing villages and liberally endowed with parks, commons and other open spaces. Good communications with London have added to its popularity and the existence of several first-class schools and many sporting facilities have also been a major factor in attracting people to the area. Although its population has increased rapidly, the District has managed to retain a pleasant leafy rural appearance. It also possesses good shopping facilities, although not on the scale of the nearby and easily reached shopping centres of Romford, Basildon and Chelmsford. With the construction of the M25, together with the A12 and the A127, the whole area is easily accessible to the major employment areas of the City, Lea Valley and the Thames Valley, as well as Chelmsford and Colchester.

The Town Centre

1. Brentwood High Street before 1840. At this time its appearance had changed little over the previous centuries. The coming of the railway a few years later was the start of a metamorphosis.

2. The Hunter Monument, erected in 1861 at High Street's junction with Ingrave Road and Ongar Road in memory of William Hunter. In 1555 he was burnt at the stake nearby for his religious beliefs.

3. High Street, looking towards Wilson's Corner at about the turn of the century. The ornate gabled building is the old post office, built in 1892 and demolished in 1938. It stood on the site of the present building at the corner of St Thomas' Road.

4. Another view of High Street about 20 years later, as seen from the opposite side of the road. Although motor cars are beginning to make an appearance, it is still pleasant for families to stroll along the pavement.

5. High Street in the 1930s. A policeman stands outside the *White Hart* and peers up the road towards Wilson's Corner.

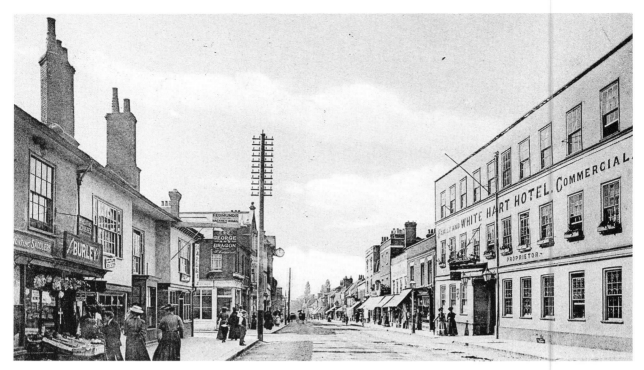

6. Another view of High Street, *c.*1900, from almost the same position but looking in the opposite direction, towards London.

7. High Street, *c.*1905. The tall classical building on the right is the former town hall, built in 1864. Sadly, this dignified building was demolished in the early 1960s and its site is now occupied by a home decorating shop. The present Council offices are in Ingrave Road.

8. The junction of High Street with Kings Road in about 1915. The junction has since been widened by the removal of the corner buildings.

9. Cyclists approach the top of Brook Street Hill in about 1900.

10. An aerial view of the centre of Brentwood, *c*.1925. The foreground shows St Thomas' church. The entire area towards the top of the picture has now been replaced by the Chapel High shopping precinct.

11. The Ongar Road/Shenfield Road junction, *c.*1935, showing Lester House, then occupied by the National Provincial Bank. The small traffic island has now been replaced by two mini roundabouts to cater for today's heavy traffic, but the buildings are almost unchanged.

12. The lower part of Kings Road looking towards Warley Road in about 1900. The small shops have long gone and have been replaced by a new office block.

13. Another view of Kings Road looking towards the railway station. In the distance is the swinging sign of the *Railway Tavern*.

14. Looking up Kings Road. The *Railway Tavern* (on the right) was a handy stop for the thirsty traveller.

15. A 'Bull-nosed' Morris passes Brentwood School and the fenced off remains of the Martyr's Oak in Ingrave Road, *c.*1930. The oak tree is reputed to mark the spot where William Hunter was put to death.

The Environs

16. This 1891 sketch of the *Fleece* at Brook Street depicts a quiet rural scene.

17. Another view of the *Fleece* a few years later with sparse traffic proceeding slowly to Brentwood.

18. Cornslands, a tranquil leafy lane at the turn of the century, one hundred yards or so from busy Brentwood railway station. Still a private road, it remains unmade today although with much more developed surroundings.

19. Priest's Lane, Shenfield, c.1900, then still a peaceful thoroughfare, although already lined with houses.

20. A lady treads warily along Worrin Road near the junction with the Parkway early this century. At that time it was just a rough track.

21. The newly built parade of shops then known as Market Place at the now busy junction of Hutton Road and Priest's Lane soon after it was built, *c*.1910. The adjacent fields have now been replaced by houses built in the inter-war period.

22. Owned by the Stratford-based firm of Young & Marten, this lorry is parked opposite a 1920s' petrol station in Rayleigh Road.

23. Shenfield Road in about 1938, then, as now, a pleasant leafy highway but almost free of traffic.

24. Queens Road, 1905: a very respectable residential street.

25. A horse and trap approaching the junction of Queens Road with Kings Road in about 1900.

26. Another turn-of-the-century view of Queens Road, with several ladies apparently making their way towards the station.

27. Rose Valley, c.1920. Today this road is characterised by a familiar row of parked vehicles on the left hand side.

28. Ingrave Road, 1905: a dusty lane during the summer months.

29. The lower part of Warley Road, *c.*1910. On the right can be seen the turreted façade of the Methodist church, built at the very end of the 19th century. The façade has since been rebuilt and the distinctive pinnacles removed.

30. This scene, postmarked 1920, depicts a much gentler era with pedestrians, cyclists and horse-drawn carts all making their way peacefully along Warley Road.

31. The Avenue, Warley, in the 1920s. Although today frequented by much more traffic, it still remains a beautiful ride through woodlands.

32.   A gathering of children in Spital Road *c*.1900, perhaps for a Sunday School outing or party, fondly watched over by their parents.

33.   Hutton Wash in about 1905 when it was a quiet country lane with no hint that it was to become a busy link to the A12 trunk road.

The Villages

34.   The village green, Blackmore, *c*.1905, still a charming area today.

35.   The *Thatchers Arms*, Great Warley, in about 1900 when it provided beer and ales from the now long defunct Hornchurch Brewery.

36. A turn-of-the-century view of the Green, Great Warley. The road leading to Tylers Common was then little more than a track.

37. Golding's Cottages and Tooks Farm, Great Warley Street. Itinerant knife sharpeners and general handymen once served local households and carried out small repairs for a few pennies.

38. Typical Essex cottages fronting Great Warley Street, c.1900. Although the general appearance remains much the same, the road now carries heavy traffic to Grays.

39. In 1905 at Herongate this horse and trap had the now busy road to Tilbury all to itself.

40. Physically, the junction of the Billericay/Brentwood Road at Herongate has changed little since this photograph was taken in about 1905 except that Brentwood Road is now part of the heavily used route from Brentwood to Tilbury and the A13. Today, there would be no prospect of walking down the centre of the road.

41. The *Crown*, Ingatestone, *c*.1910. It was in the hands of the Shuttleworth family for 60 years; they sold beer from the former Writtle Brewery. Today it is still popular and well used public house.

42. High Street, Ingatestone, 1910, looking towards Chelmsford. Superficially the overall appearance has little changed although several buildings on the right-hand side have been replaced and the beautiful trees have gone.

43. Ingatestone High Street, looking towards Market Square, in about 1910. The once well known *Spread Eagle Inn* and Posting House on the left-hand side and the terrace of cottages on the right have been replaced by modern shops.

44. The Chelmsford end of Ingatestone, c.1905, which retains much of the same tree-lined appearance today. However, the house on the right has been replaced by a small housing estate.

45. Fryerning Lane, Ingatestone, *c*.1905. After years of decay this pair of thatched cottages was well converted in the 1970s into a single house and still retains its rural appearance.

46. The Stock Road/Fryerning Lane junction, Ingatestone, 1905. The Fryerning Lane entrance remains unchanged, flanked by two sarsen stones, but Stock Road has been widened with the *Anchor* public house now on the corner.

47. Mill Green. The reverse of this card, posted in 1904, says 'This is a picture of where Mrs. Urquhart lives and that is her baby on the donkey'. Mrs. Urquart lived in one of the houses near the common.

48. Cricketers Lane, Ingrave, 1910.

49. St Nicholas' church at Ingrave, built by Robert Lord Petre in 1738, was described by Pevsner as the most remarkable 18th-century church in the county because of its massive tower and polygonal turrets.

50. The well stocked Mountnessing Stores and Post Office, c.1910. It was located near Roman Road's junction with Church Road and was replaced by new houses in about 1988.

51. Thoby Priory: a beautiful house standing in its own grounds at Mountnessing. It was demolished earlier this century and, although set in open country, parts of the grounds are now used for industrial purposes. The house took its name from a Priory founded in 1150 for Augustinian Canons which was suppressed in 1525. Arches from the former chancel and other limited remains survived until demolished with the house.

52. Mountnessing windmill in 1910, with local children watching the rotating sails. The pond in the foreground has now been replaced by ornamental gardens.

53. The infant River Wid at Mountnessing, *c*.1935: in those days a meandering stream shaded by beautiful mature trees. Today, unfortunately, most of the trees have gone and the flood plain is featureless.

54. Although photographed in 1935, South Weald remains remarkably unchanged. St Peter's, the parish church, is medieval in origin, but the substantial tower was built in 1500. The body of the church was extended in 1898 by S. S. Teulon, who also designed the nearby almshouses and National School buildings.

Open Spaces

55.   A sketch of Warley Place, then owned by the noted horticulturalist Miss Ellen Willmott. This sketch shows the Georgian eastern elevation. The walled garden provided an environment protected from the wind and frosts for early fruit and other crops – it was always several degrees warmer than outside.

56. The south elevation of Warley Place. It overlooked some of the beautiful landscaped gardens.

57. Thorndon Hall, soon after being badly damaged by fire in 1878. After being derelict for over 100 years, the centre part has now been converted into luxury flats. The Hall was built by James Paine for Lord Petre in 1770, replacing an earlier mansion sited about half a mile away.

58. A pre-war view of Weald Park. Motorists were already starting to visit the beautiful grounds but they were still able to park haphazardly, with few restrictions.

59. Weald Hall, photographed before the disastrous Second World War fire which led to its demolition in 1950. For many years it was the home of the Towers family. The older parts of the Hall were Elizabethan but in the 18th century the east block was refaced in Georgian style with the centre pediment supported on six Ionic columns.

60. Anglers at Old Hall Lake, Thorndon Park, in 1906. Samuel and Ernest Lay patiently wait for a bite. Ernest (*right*) was a bachelor, and lived with his brother and family in a house at Herongate. He was a well known part-time postman and also an amateur violinist. Today the lake is part of Thorndon Country Park, but it remains a popular spot for coarse fishing.

61. Thorndon Park Ticket No.31. This allowed the holder to collect firewood from the estate. The reverse of the card states: 'Any holder refusing to produce this Ticket, or found taking wood on any of the days not named, or breaking off wood or fences, or carrying away cut wood, acorns, chestnuts, or anything but fallen dead wood, shall forfeit the Ticket.'

See rules on back of this card

THORNDON PARK.

No. 31

The Bearer *Mrs H. Fewell*

may pick up Dead Wood on Tuesdays

and Saturdays until further notice.

October 15th 1912

62. A pre-war view of 'The Tips' at Shenfield Common. The girl is in the uniform of the County High School for Girls.

63. An attractive corner of Shenfield Common, *c.*1900, near the Ingrave Road junction. The railed off Mill Pond can be seen in the background.

64. Outside the *Foresters Inn*, Seven Arches Road, early this century. The horse has taken advantage of its owner's absence to graze the grass verge, unconcerned by passing traffic.

Commerce

65. These sturdy Edwardian bank chambers, built by the London County & Westminster Bank, stood on the site of the present NatWest Bank. The manager lived in a flat over the bank. This photograph was taken between 1909 and 1918.

66. Lloyds Bank just after it opened in the early 1930s, with the brickwork still in pristine condition.

67. The Parade cinema in Kings Road, a mecca for the film buff in pre-war days. It has now been replaced by a large office block.

68. The courtyard of the *White Hart* before the stables were converted into additional bar space and the upper galleries enclosed.

C. J. COLES,

ESSEX ARMS HOTEL

AND

RAILWAY TAVERN,

ADJOINING THE STATION,

BRENTWOOD.

J.C. Begs to return his sincere thanks for the very liberal patronage bestowed upon him, and assures his Friends and the Public that he will do all in his power to enhance the comfort of those who may favor him with a visit. He has experienced that there is but one true principle in trade—Serve your Customers as you would they should serve you—and you will find they will come again. Such is the rule laid down and carried out by C. J. COLES, of the above Hotel, where you will find every article in

WINES, SPIRITS, AND MALT LIQUORS,

Of undeniable Quality, at the Lowest possible Prices.

HUNTERS & OTHER HORSES & CARRIAGES
FOR HIRE.

FIRST-CLASS STABLING,

LOOSE BOXES, &c.

69. This fulsome advertisement for the *Essex Arms Hotel* and *Railway Tavern* appeared in 1865.

70. The old *Swan Inn* in High Street which was replaced by the present structure in about 1935.

71. The *Woolpack* public house at Fryerning, a popular Taylor Walker house because of its elevated rural setting. This photograph was taken around 1980, before extensive renovations.

CLARNICO
MARZIPAN H.

M A I
HIGH ... ES
CIGARE TES
As SMOKED By
ROYALTY & NOBILITY

ABDU...
CIGAR...

...STWARD HO...... & Co...

PLAYER'S
COUNTRY LIFE
MIXTURE of the HIGHEST CLASS

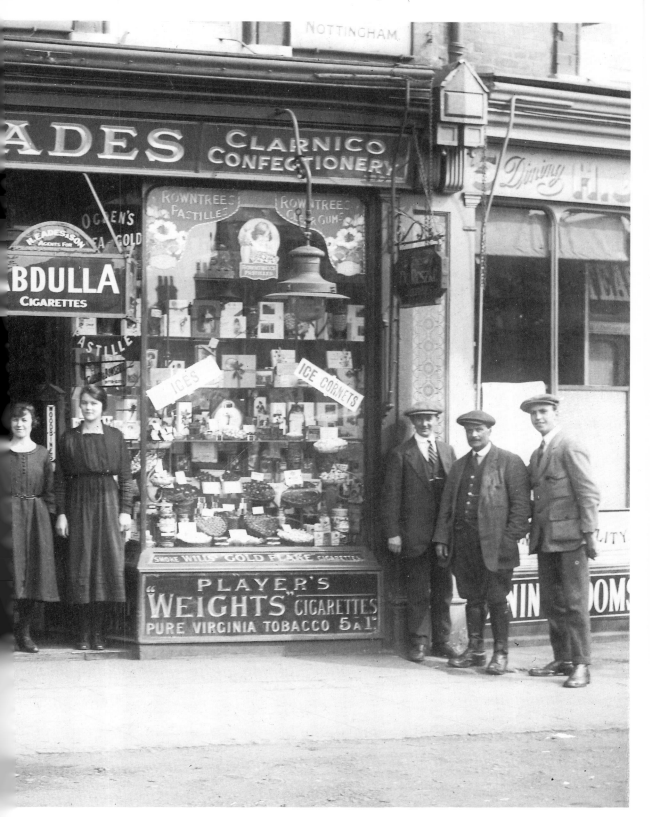

72. Three pretty assistants in the doorway of H. Eades' confectioner's and tobacconist's shop at 7 High Street, *c*.1920

73. The façade of Ellis' Radio Shop at 129 High Street in about 1930, dressed up to resemble a contemporary cottage.

74. Thomas Ellis standing beside his delivery van, decorated to enter the 1933 Brentwood Carnival procession.

75. A pre-war view of Rippon Bros. motor showrooms in High Street, now a shopping arcade.

76. Woolworth's, the 3d. and 6d. department store, built their small branch in Brentwood in the 1930s on the south side of High Street, west of the Chapel ruins. In post-war days it was replaced by a considerably larger store further along High Street on the opposite side of the road. This, in turn, closed in the 1970s when the company made huge losses nationwide and closed a number of branches. A shop selling furniture now occupies the original premises.

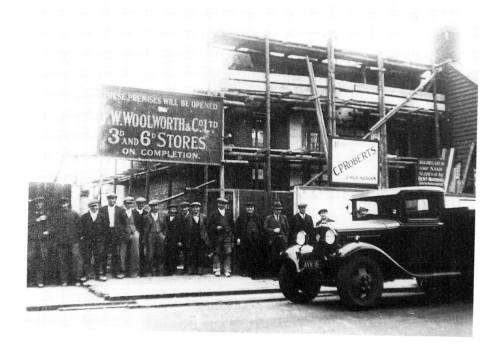

BRENTWOOD.

J. M. WARD,

LINENDRAPER, SILK-MERCER,

HOSIER, HABERDASHER,

LACEMAN, AND GLOVER,

ONE DOOR FROM THE WHITE HART INN, BRENTWOOD,

INVITES his Friends and the Public to INSPECT HIS STOCK, suitable for the present Season.

SHAWLS, MANTLES, AND DRESSES,

Of the Newest Designs in every novel Fabric.

SHEETINGS, COUNTERPANES, BLANKETS, AND BED TICKS.

French Merinoes, Winceys, Prints, Linens, Calicoes, Long Cloths, and Flannels,

OF THE VERY BEST MAKE, AT THE LOWEST MARKET PRICES.

GLOVES, HOSIERY,

PLAIN AND FANCY;

STAYS, UMBRELLAS, &c., &c.

A LARGE ASSORTMENT OF

LADIES' AND CHILDREN'S BOOTS AND SHOES.

FAMILY MOURNING Good and Cheap.

AGENT FOR THE

United Kingdom Temperance and General Provident Institution for Life Insurance, and for the "Royal" Fire Office.

---

77. This advertisement, giving details of the wide-ranging stock held by Mr. J. M. Ward's drapery near the *White Hart Hotel*, High Street, appeared in the 1865 edition of the *Essex Almanac*.

Education

78.   Brentwood School House in 1847, today known as Old Big House. This well-proportioned and detailed sketch was drawn by W. W. Brown, aged ten.

79.   An aerial view of Brentwood School in 1925. In front of the school St Helen's Roman Catholic Cathedral can just be seen.

80. The main Brentwood School buildings fronting Ingrave Road. This postcard was sent in August 1914 by Horace Fox who informs his father, 'This is the place where C. Company and the Machine Gun Section are Billeted. Our Section sleep in the corridor behind the Main Entrance. We are expecting to go to Birmingham or Manchester soon.'

81. Roden House early this century, when used as Brentwood School's boarding house and Preparatory School. It is now the home of the headmaster.

82. Passers-by were probably quite unaware that these beautiful gardens existed behind Old Big School in 1925. Croquet used to be played on this lawn but additional classrooms have since been built on some of the gardens.

83.   The interior of Old Big School at the turn of the century. The old iron stove on the right was the centre of school life, where boys gathered for news, gossip and warmth. Some of the old desk tops, deeply notched with graffiti, have now been incorporated in walls and window ledges.

SIR ANTHONY BROWNE'S SCHOOL, BRENTWOOD.

Report _Mich^s_ Term, 1903.

Name _E. E. Reed_ terts   Form _II._   Division _3_

Form III 12th of 26 boys	LATIN	- -	7th place. Writing poor. Work always careful – & improving
	FRENCH	- -	21st Fair at times: tries.
	GERMAN	-	
Division 3 7th of 25 boys	ENG. SUBJECTS		6th good – except writing.
	MATHEMATICS	-	9th promising – works hard.
	SCIENCE	-	6th good –
	GREEK	- - - -	
	DRAWING	- - - -	13th 1 25 boys. fair –
	SHORTHAND	- - - -	good.
	MUSIC	- - - -	
	HEAD MASTER'S REMARKS	-	Very creditable.

Next term will begin with Chapel Service at 10 a.m., on _Frid. Jan 22_

It is requested that all boys attend the Opening Service of term.

84. A 1903 school report, during the time the Revd. Edwin Bean was headmaster. A wide variety of academic subjects were taught.

85. Before the Great War, bare furnishings and patriotic decorations were a feature of a boarder's study.

86. Brentwood was one of the first schools in the country to build a swimming pool, in 1864. This picture, taken in 1911, shows the second pool which was on what is now Library Square.

87. A school group in about 1875. In the centre is Revd. William Quennell, headmaster between 1870 and 1879.

88.   The cast of *The Critic*, 1903. The tradition of producing fine costume drama continues.

89.   The 1903-4 Brentwood School football team. Earlier, in the 1860s, Brentwood schoolboys played different kinds of football, varying the rules. A new master, the Revd. Francis, encouraged them to stick to soccer and actually captained the team in the late 1860s.

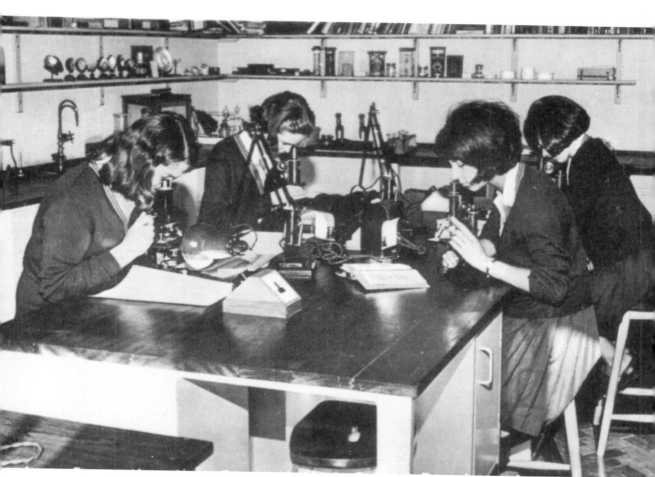

90.   The well equipped zoology room at the Ursuline Convent High School prior to 1960.

91.   Girls at the Ursuline Convent School listen attentively to their science teacher, *c.*1960.

92.   The original Art Room at the Ursuline Convent School.

93. The sisters of the Ursuline Convent (far left) supervise croquet early this century.

94. The County High School for Girls soon after it opened in 1927.

95. This carefully posed photograph, taken in about 1900, shows pupils of Christ Church School staring curiously at the camera.

Industry

96. The now defunct Fielders Brewery in Kings Road supplied beer and ales to many local public houses. Now only the tap room survives. This photograph was taken in about 1910.

HILL'S
BRENTWOOD BREWERY.

GOOD BEER IS LIQUID BREAD.

PALE

ALE

	BAR.	KIL.	FIR.
X	27s.	13s. 6d.	6s. 9d.
K	32s.	16s. 0d.	8s. 0d.
KK	40s.	20s. 0d.	10s. 0d.
XXXX	54s.	27s. 0d.	13s. 6d.
Pale Ale	54s.	27s. 0d.	13s. 6d.
Porter	36s.	18s. 0d.	9s. 0d.

97. An 1865 advertisement for Hill's Brewery in Myrtle Road, which was later sold to Ind Coope of Romford.

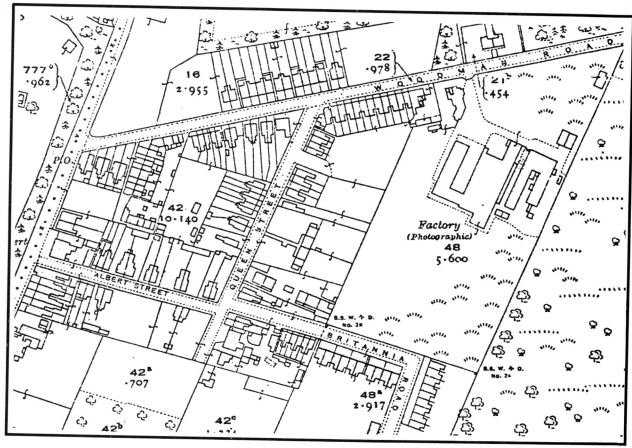

98. A 1920 map of the first Warley factory of Ilford Ltd.

99. The original Ilford Ltd. factory in 1920, as seen from Britannia Road. Many of these buildings remained until 1975.

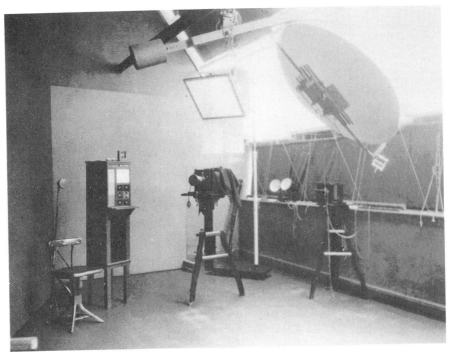

100. The Selo film testing department, which opened in 1938. The firm employed many young women on this work.

101. An aerial view of Rotary Hoes' extensive factory at West Horndon in 1950. This firm played a significant role in mechanising British agriculture. The factory is now subdivided into units occupied by different firms.

102. Herongate Forge in Billericay Road, *c.*1910. The two men are W. D. Dickerson (left) and A. Carrol.

Transport

103.   Brentwood railway station, prior to the duplication of the tracks in 1934. City ladies and gents await the next London train.

104.   Another view of Brentwood station. The Liverpool Street train approaches from Shenfield.

105. Rayleigh Road and Shenfield railway station in about 1908. The booking hall and station master's house on the right were demolished to make way for the building shown in the following picture.

106. Shenfield station, *c.*1935. The rebuilding of the station and a new bridge to take additional tracks took place concurrently. Recently further additions to the station have been made.

107. The original 'Up' and 'Down' platforms at Shenfield station, numbered 2 and 3, in about 1910, before there were through trains to Southend. Passengers for that branch had to transfer to the platform on the extreme right, now number 1. Platforms 4 and 5 were built when the additional tracks were laid.

108. A steam engine on the Shenfield turntable, 26 March 1913. The turntable was dismantled when the line was electrified, and a car park now occupies the site.

109. The Hook Continental Express, drawn by *Lord Roberts*, speeds through Shenfield on its way to London. The journey from Harwich to Liverpool Street took about 1½ hours at the time this photograph was taken around 1950.

110. The Clacton-on-Sea to Liverpool Street train pulls away from Ingatestone station on 7 May 1910.

111. A Leyland 'Lion', run by the City Coach Company, at the bus stop in High Street in about 1935, on its way to Laindon.

112. A diagram of the bus services from Brentwood once operated by 'City'.

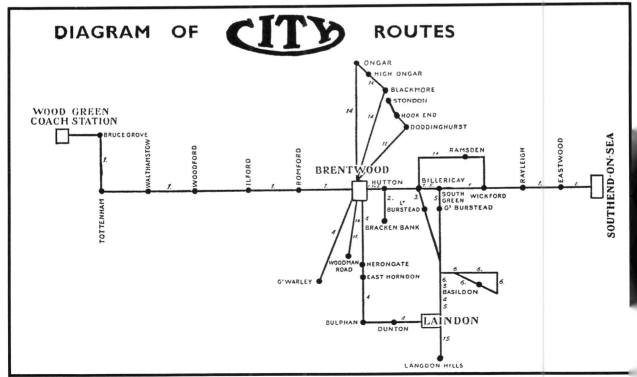

DIAGRAM OF **CITY** ROUTES

WOOD GREEN
COACH STATION

BRUCE GROVE

ONGAR
HIGH ONGAR
BLACKMORE
STONDON
HOOK END
DODDINGHURST

RAMSDEN

TOTTENHAM   WALTHAMSTOW   WOODFORD   ILFORD   ROMFORD   BRENTWOOD   HUTTON   BILLERICAY   RAYLEIGH   EASTWOOD

SOUTHEND-ON-SEA

LT BURSTEAD
BRACKEN BANK

SOUTH GREEN   WICKFORD
G' BURSTEAD

WOODMAN ROAD   HERONGATE
G'WARLEY   EAST HORNDON

BASILDON

BULPHAN   LAINDON
DUNTON

LANGDON HILLS

113. 'Regent' was one of the small bus companies in Brentwood.
The firm was taken over by 'City' in 1936. The front of an Eastern
National bus, its driver in the uniform white coat, can just be seen.

**Revised Time Table—To be operated
on and after February 9th, 1932.**
This cancels all previous Time Tables.

REGENT
MOTOR SERVICE

**Brentwood Station, Warley
Woodman Road, Pilgrims
Hatch & Canterbury Tye.**

The Proprietors cannot be responsible for exact
adherence to times of Buses though every effort
will be made to maintain them.

Your Suggestions and Comments will be wel-
comed and will receive Personal Attention.

'Phone: F. H. FULLER,
Brentwood   242, Ongar Road,
382.   Brentwood.

114. The front cover of the timetable issued by 'Regent' in 1932.
The proprietor was then able to offer a 'personal' service to the
travelling public.

115. This smart six-wheeled single-decker was one of 12 purchased by 'City' in 1937 for local use.

116.   The 'City' bus park in about 1948, with assorted vehicles of varying ages. It was subsequently occupied by the Eastern National, whose southern services were renamed Thamesbury Buses in October 1990.

117.   This curious little bus parked near Wilson's Corner was purchased by the Brentwood & District Bus Company in September 1935 and passed to 'City' when they acquired the firm.

118. Leyland double-deckers entered the 'City' fleet in 1947 and were used on the Southend to Wood Green run.

119. This diagram showing the various bus and rail services was issued as part of a comprehensive monthly timetable prior to World War Two.

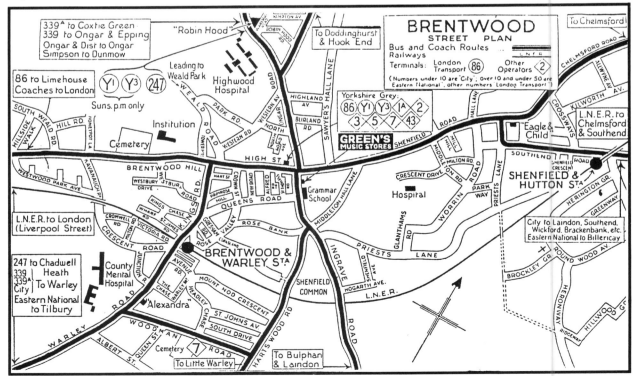

120.   A collection of cars photographed on the forecourt of No.47 High Street in the 1930s. Today Lloyds Bank occupies the site.

121.   The Shenfield Road petrol station in 1949. A Standard Vanguard, one of the most successful immediate post-war cars, is being filled with petrol.

122.   Leonard Pitts proudly displays his brand new delivery van in about 1920.

123. A 'Selo' van, c.1935.

124. A high-wing monoplane advertising 'Selo' film in the 1930s.

125. A typical open lorry of the 1930s. This vehicle was originally a bus owned by 'City'. Its body was removed when transferred to the Brentwood Engineering Company.

Public Buildings and Services

126. An artist's impression of the Chapel of St Thomas à Becket, founded in 1226, as viewed from High Street. It was demolished towards the end of the last century. In 1835 a new church was built and that was replaced in 1883 by the existing one.

127. A Sunday School party assembles in front of Christ Church, Warley Road, in about 1910.

128. Built in 1892 and influenced by Dutch architecture, this post office was replaced in 1938 by the present Georgian-style building.

129. Ingatestone post office at the turn of the century. The postmistress, flanked by two telegraph boys, stands in the doorway. These premises are now used as a ladies boutique. A new village post office was built further up the High Street in 1916 and remains in use.

130. An aerial view of Warley Hospital, surrounded by well-maintained gardens, in about 1920.

131. The original Brentwood District Hospital at Shenfield Common, prior to 1930.

132.   Brentwood District Hospital, soon after it opened in 1934. The young trees have since grown and now screen the hospital from Crescent Road.

133.   Highwood Schools, Ongar Road, built by the Metropolitan Asylum's Board in 1904 for sick children.

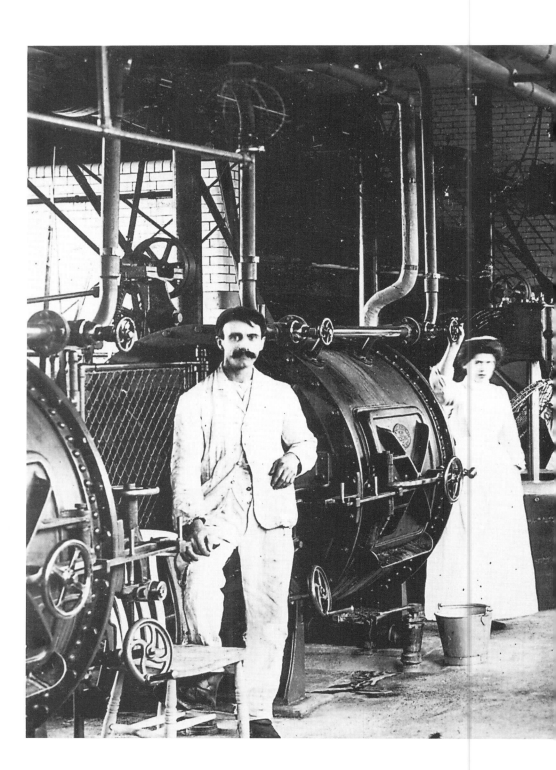

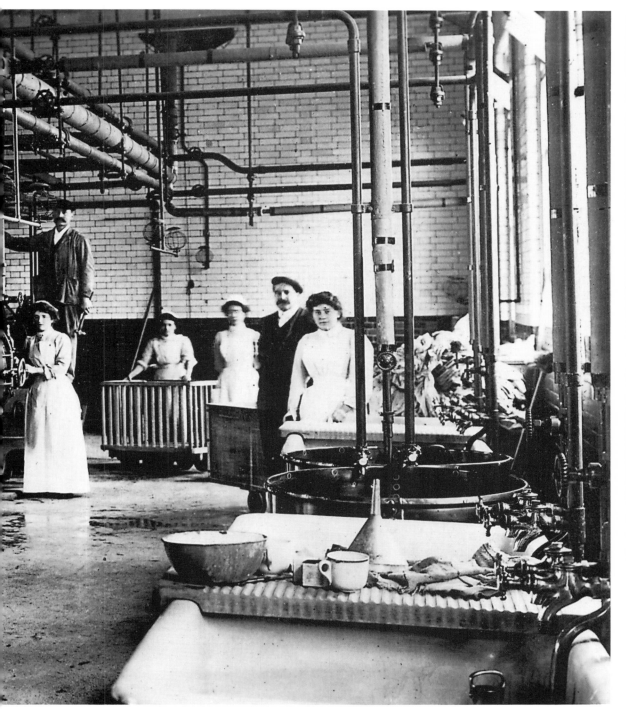

134.   Like most large institutions Highwood Schools had their own laundry. It is seen here a few years after the school was built.

135. Brentwood's former outdoor swimming pool in the 1930s.

136. The South Essex Waterworks Company's pumping station at Warley in about 1900. It supplied the first mains water to the town.

137. Hutton Industrial School, 1909. It was built by the Poplar Board of Guardians in 1906 for the sum of £160,000 to give East London boys a healthy rural environment.

138.   Brentwood firemen in full uniform, with their horse-drawn appliance, *c.*1910.

139. Ingatestone firemen outside their station in Fryerning Lane in about 1950, with their Bedford appliance. All the firemen were locally employed, a practice which continues today at the present station in High Street, although the custom of calling the men out by siren has been discontinued.

140. A studio portrait of Constable Ernest Marriage, soon after moving to Brentwood in 1912.

The Army

141.   An artist's impression of General Parker reviewing the troops at Warley Common, 1779.

142.   A sketch of the tented camp the same year.

143. 'The Pompadours', the 1st Battalion, Essex Regiment, on parade at Warley Barracks in 1902 on their return from South Africa.

THE HIGHEST BOUNTY IN
NATIONAL BANK NOTES,
OR,
HARD
GUINEAS.

56th Regt.

MAJOR KEATING,
Now wants Sixty Men of Spirit and Enterprise to
COMPLETE THE
Fifty-sixth Regiment,
Or, OLD SAUCY POMPADOURS.
Any Lads chusing to follow the Honorable Profession of a Soldier,
may Apply at the Sign of the
FIGHTING COCKS, RATHKEALE.
The MAJOR begs to remind his Countrymen of the preference
already given, by One Hundred and Sixty County Limerick
and Kerry Lads, who have joined the
POMPADOUR STANDARD,
And he hopes for a continuance of that partiality which he has
to amply experienced.

144. This enlistment poster invited recruits to join the 56th Regiment,
which in 1881 became the 1st Battalion the Essex Regiment.

145.   An aerial view of Warley Barracks immediately after World War Two.

146.   Barrack Road, now Eagle Way, early this century. The field guns mark the entrance to the Barracks.

147. The Depot Officers' Mess, *c.*1914. It is still occupied by the War Department although the army has left Warley.

148. Men of the regiment marching off the parade ground at the end of a square-bashing session, *c.*1915.

149. This group of recruits was photographed outside the Barracks in February 1916 prior to active service postings the following month.

150. Soldiers relaxing outside the quartermaster's stores in about 1915.

151. This extract from Pte. Eric Boesch's paybook shows enlistment into National Service at Warley on 29 August 1946. He was discharged with the rank of Lance Corporal two years later, after serving in the Royal Army Ordnance Corps.

(1) SOLDIER'S NAME and DESCRIPTION on ATTESTATION.

Army Number *19056447*

Surname (in capitals) *BOESCH*

Christian Names (in full) *ERIC*

Date of Birth *20.4.28*

Trade on Enlistment *Analytical Chemist*

Religious Denomination *C/E*

Approved Society

Membership No.

Enlisted at *Warley* On *29.8.46*

For the :—

NS ACT FOR DURATION OF EMERGENCY.
* Strike out those inapplicable.

For _____ years with the Colours and _____ years in the Reserve.

Signature of Soldier *E Boesch*

Date *29th August 1946*

DESCRIPTION ON ENLISTMENT.

Height *5* ft. *11* ins. Weight *125* lbs.
Maximum Chest *34½* ins. Complexion *Pale*
Eyes *Brown* Hair *Brown*
Distinctive Marks and Minor Defects:
Mole R/ side

7/10/46 A and S. G. *76c*

A & S Group DIS

CONDITION ON TRANSFER TO RESERVE.

Found fit for

Defects or History of past illness which should be enquired into if called up for Service.

AFW3149 COMPLETED
DATE *16-8-48*
MED. CAT. *B1*

Date _____ 19 ____
Initials of M.O. i/c.

152. A newly enlisted National Serviceman smartly presents arms to Field Marshal Lord Montgomery during his inspection of the Barracks in 1947.

153. A pretty young A.T.S. private from Warley sat for this studio portrait at H. Blunkell's studios at No.4 High Street in the early 1940s, wearing her best uniform and non-regulation side hat.

154. An aerial view of the extensive wartime R.E.M.E. depot at The Drive. The site has now been redeveloped as a business park.

Events

155.   On 4 September 1909 fire gutted the premises of Wilson's Great Eastern Stores. Although the fire brigade arrived promptly, the Water Company reputedly failed to respond to the emergency until some hours had elapsed, at which time the mains were fully opened. The store was subsequently rebuilt in a more substantial form. The building is now occupied by a furniture salesroom but the road junction is still known as Wilson's Corner.

156. Crowds gather in the High Street to celebrate the coronation of King George V in 1910.

157. In 1911 an army 'Beta' airship, piloted by Capt. Edward Matland, 3rd Militia Bn., Essex Regiment, landed at Warley Common and this little craft was the subject of much interest. Among the visitors were two local girls, Grace and Thiza Ellis, seen in the foreground of this photograph. Shortly afterwards, Capt. Matland transferred to the Royal Engineers, eventually becoming an Air Commodore in the R.A.F. He was killed at the age of 41 on 24 August 1921, when the R38 Airship crashed in Yorkshire.

158. The Essex Union Hunt meet at Shenfield Common in 1921.

159. In 1927 the Essex Federation of Women's Institutes held an Historical Pageant at Chelmsford. Among those taking part was the Thorndon Group W.I. whose tableau depicted Lady Alicia Tyrell and her children.

MINISTRY OF FOOD.

SUGAR REGISTRATION CARD.

E   665425

C. Name *Savill Henry Norman*

Address *Kelvedon Corner*

Brentwood

Retailer with whom the Householder has registered:—

D. Signature of Retailer *Salisbury Durrant*

Address *Brentwood*

..5.. No. of persons *five* .... Initials *H.N.*

District ONGAR.

S. 2.

(20834). Wt. 26143/G90. 2,600,000. 8/17. McC. & Co., Ltd. (E 1655).

This part to be kept by the Householder.

MINISTRY OF FOOD.

R 2.

RATIONING ORDER, 1918.

PURCHASER'S SHOPPING CARD.

MEAT.

This Card is valid only with the Butcher who issued it, and whose name appears below. If you change your Butcher, a new Card will be issued by the new Butcher.

A   BUTCHER'S NAME AND ADDRESS.

Your Butcher must stamp his name and address below before issue, otherwise the card will not be valid.

W. O. KNIGHTBRIDGE,

KELVEDON HATCH,

BRENTWOOD.

B   PURCHASER'S NAME AND ADDRESS.

N. Savill Esq

Old Crown

Kelvedon Hatch

THIS CARD IS VALID ONLY WITH THE BUTCHER WITH WHOM THE RATION CARDS OF MEMBERS OF THE HOUSEHOLD HAVE BEEN DULY REGISTERED.

(33921) Wt. 42573 17,002,500 8-19 W B & L

---

160 & 161. During both World Wars food was strictly rationed and everyone was required to register with individual shops to obtain their share. In 1916 Henry Savill of Kelvedon Corner had elected to purchase his sugar from Salisbury Durrant's, whilst for meat he was registered with W. C. Knightbridge.

P 1105 L   GENERAL POST OFFICE   Duplicate

BILLETING OF CIVILIAN POPULATION

RECEIVED from the Postmaster-General the sum

of .... Pounds .... Shillings

.... Pence being "Billeting" payments for

.... weeks ⎰ .... Adults.

.... ⎱ .... Children.

£	s	d
—	6	6

Signature of Payee *M Barton*

Address of Billet ....

NOTE.—Duplicate receipt forms must be detached and forwarded daily to the Local Billeting Officer.

Stamp of Paying Office.

---

162. In the Second World War children were evacuated from London and other major cities. For a time, children were moved to Brentwood and billeted in private houses. An allowance of 10s. 6d. per week per child was given to the occupier.

163. Carnivals are traditionally an important part of summer entertainment throughout the district. In 1921 Mr. and Mrs. Caton and their nephew, Robert Ellis, entered the Brentwood carnival procession as 'Pip, Squeak and Wilfred', three popular newspaper cartoon characters of the time.

164. A flying bomb crashed in Hill Road on 15 June 1944 injuring ten people and destroying two houses. The following morning the army helped to recover household belongings from the debris.

People

165. Revd. Edwin Bean, headmaster of Brentwood School 1891-1913. Under his guidance the school roll grew from a mere 46 to 225 boys.

166. Engagement photograph of Cpl. E. Marriage of the Military Mounted Police to Miss Florence Flutter in 1916. Prior to joining the army Cpl. Marriage had been a Brentwood police constable. Miss Flutter's family ran a well known confectionery shop in High Street.

167a. & b. The much loved Revd. H. D. Heatley, Rector of Ingrave 1843-1909, with his wife. These photographs were probably taken around 1852.

168. Charles and Eliza Felton, two Herongate characters photographed in 1906 on Eliza's 50th birthday. They lived for most of their lives in a small cottage in Brentwood Road where they raised 11 children.

169. Henry, John, Albert, Thomas and Arthur, the five sons of Charles and Eliza Felton, photographed in 1913 in the back garden of Barrack Row, Herongate.

170. Mr. E. King, stationmaster at Brentwood railway station at the turn of the century.

171. Superintendent David Scott (*centre*) and his men at Brentwood police station in 1918. Included within the group are two women special constables, the first employed in Essex. The county did not have regular policewomen until 1940.

THIS IS PRETYMAN DAY

172. Miss Nancy Crofton Savill (*left*) and Miss Viola Quenell campaign for the Conservative candidate in a parliamentary election just prior to the Great War.

173.   A group picture of the 1st Warley Company of the Boys Brigade taken in a garden at Fryerning in 1909.

174. The Warley Mental Hospital's football team proudly display their trophies in about 1930.

175. The now defunct Ingrave and East Horndon Brass Band, c.1909.

176. A 1930s' Brentwood School cricket team pose for this picture outside the school buildings. The School's first recorded cricket match was played in 1854.

177. The immaculately dressed Selo ladies tennis team of 1937-38. Sporting and social activities were encouraged by the firm.

178.   A 1938 wedding day picture of L/Cpl. Baker and his bride with other part-time soldiers of the Essex Yeomanry. Most of those seen here later served with distinction in the Middle and Far East.

Bibliography

Baker, W. J., *A History of the Marconi Company*.
Burrows, J., *The Essex Militia*.
Burrow, J., Ltd., *The County Handbook*.
Crawley, R. J., *et al*, *The Years Between 1909-69* Vols. I & II.
Coe, R. A., *A Postcard from Ingatestone.The Essex Almanac* (1865).
Gordon, D. I., *Regional History of Railways of Great Britain*.
Hercock, R. J., and Jones, G. A., *Silver by the Ton*.
Javis, S. A., and Harrison, C. T., *In Search of Essex*.
Javis, S. A., *Victorian & Edwardian Essex*.
Lewis, R. R., *History of Brentwood School*.
Le Lievre, A., *Miss Willmott of Warley Place*.
Mckerness, M. G., *Brentwood County High School*.
Martin, Col. T. A., M.B.E., *The Essex Regiment 1929-50*.
Osborne, A., and Snell, P., *The City Coach Company*.
Pevsner, Nikolaus, *The Buildings of England*.
Ramsey, W. R., *The Battle of Britain Then and Now*.
Scarfe, N., *Essex*
Simpson, F. D., *Brentwood in Old Picture Postcards* Vols I & II.
Survey of Ingatestone High Street, I.F.H.A.S.
Ward, G. A., *Brentwood*.
Ward, G. A., *A History of South Weald and Brentwood*.
Warley – 25 Years Silver Jubilee, Ford booklet.
White, William, *County of Essex*, 1845.

Leaflets
Essex County Council, *Thorndon Country Park*.
Essex County Council, *Weald Country Park*.
Essex County Council, *Introduction to Ingatestone Hall*.
The Marillac.

Newspapers
Various issues of:
Brentwood Gazette.
Brentwood District News.
Brentwood Weekly News.